Toxic and Intoxicating: Puritan Theology and the Thirst for Power

Dr Matthew Rowley

The Latimer Trust

ISBN 978-1-906327-56-9

Cover photo: Frederick Chapman, 'The perils of our forefathers' (New
York: Joseph Laing, 1859). The lithograph is in the American
Antiquarian Society (Lithfff Chap Lain Peri). Photo by Matthew Rowley,
2016. The original painting hangs in the Forbes Library in Northampton
Massachusetts.

Published by the Latimer Trust April 2019.

The Latimer Trust (formerly Latimer House, Oxford) is a conservative
Evangelical research organisation within the Church of England, whose
main aim is to promote the history and theology of Anglicanism as
understood by those in the Reformed tradition. Interested readers are
welcome to consult its website for further details of its many activities.

The Latimer Trust

London N14 4PS UK

Registered Charity: 1084337

Company Number: 4104465

Web: www.latimertrust.org

E-mail: administrator@latimertrust.org

I would like to thank Lee Gatiss and Benedict Bird for providing valuable feedback on this lecture.

1. Introduction

'How does it feel to be wrong?' This is what the journalist Kathryn Schulz asked her audience in a 2011 TED talk. 'Dreadful. Thumbs down. Embarrassing', they replied. She then told them that they answered the *wrong* question. She did not ask 'How does it feel to *realize* you're wrong?' The audience laughed, but her point was serious. Being wrong, in the moment, '*feels* like being right'.[1]

As a historian, I generally avoid saying that historical persons or movements were *wrong*. I am not qualified – let alone equipped – to do so. There are too many historical unknowns. Difficulties multiply when judging complex beliefs from a distance. My concern is not that of the theologian, declaring a doctrine right or wrong. When can a historian say that beliefs were wrong? Perhaps when those convictions involved predictions that fail to materialise?

We might, for example, ask the following question: What did the Puritans *think God was doing* through their political and military efforts? We might then examine some historical claims. Was God establishing the New Jerusalem in New England, as argued by John Eliot in *The Christian Commonwealth* (1659)? Would this New Jerusalem be located in England, as Richard Baxter anticipated in *A Holy Commonwealth* (1659)? Were the British Civil Wars eschatologically-significant events that ushered in the global reign of Christ as the godly triumphed over all ungodly polities, as heralded by John Owen in *The advantage of the kingdom of Christ* (1651)?

These examples come from the period after the execution of Charles I. The claims have the added benefit of being (to some degree) testable. Despite the durability of the American hubris, colonial New England did not see the New Jerusalem established among the Native Americans. The Restoration tempered hopes for a British Jerusalem. And Puritan armies did not topple Rome or bring all the Catholic powers to their knees. We can reasonably say these claims were wrong, even though the claimant earnestly believed they were right. Additionally, after the Restoration, Baxter, Eliot, and Owen distanced themselves from their confident theo-political speculations. Theology twice staggered under

---

1. 'Kathryn Schulz, 'On Being Wrong' (26 April 2011). Online: https://www.ted.com/talks/kathryn_schulz_on_being_wrong?language=en. Retrieved 4 March 2019. Italics added.

the influence of politics, first when these claims were made and second when they were retracted.

My aim here is not to pontificate on Puritan errors. I intend to illustrate the effect of political and military stress on their theology. I make a simple point: the thirst for power changed Puritan theology, often in ways that went unnoticed. The rise and decline of political puritanism afforded unique theological temptations. As victors or victims, many approached cultural conflict with a deep sense their cause was righteous.

Beliefs normally bend and sway under the influence of politics. Victimisation, marginalisation and failure can be a potent mixture, as will be described later. However, the belief in righteousness – especially when amplified by success – can prove intoxicating. In the autobiography of Christopher Hitchens, the famed Atheist reflected on the activism of his youth:

> 'A consciousness of rectitude can be a terrible thing, and in those days I didn't just think that I was right: I thought that "we"... were being damn well *proved* right. If you have never yourself had the experience of feeling that you are yoked to the great steam engine of history, then allow me to inform you that the conviction is a very intoxicating one'.[2]

We will be looking at the darker moments of Puritan history. Like Hitchens, 'A consciousness of rectitude' usually preceded controversial actions. Like Hitchens, many thought their righteousness was being '*proved* right' by events. Like Hitchens, they felt 'yoked to the great steam engine of history' and found it 'very intoxicating'.

I must first explore the importance of self-critique to the writing of history before providing an overview of political puritanism. I then offer nine thematic sketches of puritan theology under the pressure of politics and war. I conclude by attempting to balance the portrait of puritanism sketched here by emphasizing that the thirst for power was only a part of their rich and varied history.

---

2. Christopher Hitchens, *Hitch-22: A Memoir* (New York: Twelve, 2010), 98.

2. History and Self-Critique

My appreciation for Puritan theology drew me to a seminary where that tradition was critically taught and cherished. As I took more classes on Reformed thought – particularly that of Jonathan Edwards – I came to notice that many Puritans had two ways of interacting with Scripture and articulating providential beliefs. There was a peace mentality and a wartime mentality. Theologians shifted from cautious to confident providentialism. Politics and war exerted a powerful strain on their thinking. In sum, in stressful military or political situations, the Puritans used Scripture in ways that their peacetime selves would have disagreed with. The theology of Jonathan Edwards or John Owen, for example, shifted under stress. These profound shifts in their thinking were likely unintentional and went, to a large extent, unnoticed – and for that reason the drink was more potent. *They* did not think their theology staggered under the influence of politics.

How are we to interact with historical inconsistencies like this? Our judgements should be adorned with sympathy, anchored by humility, and sharpened by self-critique – otherwise the historian risks descent into self-righteousness. I could have chosen to study violent Islamists or Atheists – and there would have been an abundance of fascinating source material. However, I chose to study darker moments in Protestant history, in part, to counteract my own bent towards self-righteousness.

In *Protestants: The Faith that Made the Modern World*, Alec Ryrie warned of some dangers in historical critique:

> 'I have written about a very wide range of religious movements. I find some of them admirable, some of them repellent, and some of them tinged with madness. In each case, I have tried to treat them with sympathy. This is not because I myself believe that witches should be put to death or that apartheid is God's will. It is because earnest, God-fearing Protestants who were no more inherently wicked than you or I did believe these things, even at the same time as other Protestants passionately opposed them. Condemning ugly beliefs is easy, but it is also worth the effort to understand why people once believed them. If we are lucky, later ages

3

might be as indulgent toward us. We all live in glass houses. Those who are without sin are welcome to cast the first stone'.[1]

It is easy to notice specks in the eyes of previous generations and difficult to let their examples point out beams in our own.

A second danger relates to the purpose of historical reflection. History often functions as a tool of politics. Take, for example, centuries of Protestant historians who wrote Irish history, in part, to exclude Irish Catholics from civil or religious rights.[2] It would be naïve for me to suppose this essay is apolitical, for it is my desire that Christians come to terms with their past.

Historical critique seems more difficult for some Protestants. My aim, however, is not to win a political or cultural war. I aim to show how fighting this war often leads to a shift in the very beliefs that one claims to cherish, protect, and promote. Involvement with politics is, to some degree, unavoidable. Christians, historically, have taken many different stances – ranging from fight to flight. Each stance comes with benefits and risks for the vitality of the state and the purity of the church. Consider this a health warning.

Having stated a few pitfalls, historical analysis also holds forth many promises. Daniel Neal, an eighteenth-century historian of the Puritans, said this of their quest for power:

> 'Nor can there be any inconvenience in remembering the mistakes of our ancestors, when all the parties concerned are gone off the stage... but it may be of some use and benefit to mankind by enabling them to avoid those *rocks* on which their forefathers have split'.[3]

1. Alec Ryrie, *Protestants: The Faith that Made the Modern World* (London: William Collins, 2017), 11.
2. For excellent essays on this, see Mark Empey, Alan Ford and Miriam Moffitt (eds.), *The Church of Ireland and Its Past: History, Interpretation and Identity* (Dublin: Four Courts, 2017).
3. Daniel Neal, *The history of the Puritans, or, Protestant non-conformists, ... with an account of their principles* (Dublin, 1755) II:viii.

The irony is that Christians in the present have largely forgotten what Neal was 'remembering'. This is particularly true when remembering the clergy who participated in politics and war. For example, John Owen is remembered for his exegesis and Christology. The church has largely forgotten his apocalyptically-aggressive advocacy of war. The church, in other words, has forgotten the brutal piety of John Owen in his political intoxication.

Had John Owen preached an Arminian view of soteriology, Reformed publishers might never have reproduced his works. However, Owen preached some astonishing things against Episcopalians and Scottish Presbyterians – and those comments were quarantined in volume eight of his collected works where the church has largely forgotten about them. Like Daniel Neal, I agree there is no 'inconvenience in remembering the mistakes of our ancestors'.

Neal then said remembrance 'may be of some use and benefit to mankind by enabling them to avoid those *rocks* on which their forefathers have split'. Protestants, however, have largely done the opposite. Many turned that age – the age of Owen, the Pilgrims, the founding of America, and the Westminster Assembly – into the golden age where Christians really lived based on the Bible. They have glorified some of 'those *rocks* on which their forefathers have split'.

Second, valorising the Puritans – if not done in ways that seriously engage their failings – can do more harm than good. This is because some engaged in the culture wars want to return to the greener pastures of the seventeenth and eighteenth centuries. However, these fields were made verdant by memory. This was an impressive time for theology, but not for repentance over violence. The age was marked by the pursuit of truth, but that truth was often decoupled from charity. Their scholarship was remarkable for exegesis, but a toxic mixture of politics permeated much theology. They were Christians who longed to build the kingdom of God, but many thought God would accomplish it through the violence of man.

After years of studying the darker moments of their history, I am in awe of the Puritans. *Awe*, as a term, encompasses both admiration and horror; respect and revulsion. I have tried to get inside their heads to understand *how* they saw their actions: not as encroaching shadows but as the inbreaking of shafts of light. In other words, what looks to me like a stain on their reputation, many wore as a badge of honour.

Critique is integral to Scripture, as noted by Rabbi Lord Jonathan Sacks: 'The Hebrew Bible is the supreme example of that rarest of phenomena, a national literature of self-criticism'.[4] The Puritans continued this narrative of self-critique through their regular fast days. They were also adept at critiquing persons and ideas in Christian history. Although some Christians have had a blinkered view of the past, there is also a long history of reassessment, critique, and confession. In an age of political polarisation, it is important to resist simplified versions of groups – present or past. Perhaps wrestling with the ambiguities of history can foster caution and self-critique in the present.

---

4. Jonathan Sacks, *Not in God's Name: Confronting Religious Violence* (London: Hodder & Stoughton, 2015), 53.

3. Overview of Political Puritanism

My research focuses on Puritan theology before, during, and after war.[1] I have given the term 'godly violence' to their belief that killing was both just and holy. The killing itself was thought to be *godly*. Additionally, 'godly violence' was killing performed – they thought – by God himself or by the Puritans (who preferred to be called 'the godly').

Belief-formation is a second research focus. How did the godly form the belief that their cause was just or holy? How did they arrive at the conclusion that God was on their side? What did they make of contrary evidence? The godly thought God communicated through bloodshed, and there was a battle for the interpretation of his combat communications. I have given the term 'military providentialism' to this struggle to rightly interpret and articulate God's will and agency in war. My research examines 'godly violence' and 'military providentialism' by focusing on Puritan beliefs about killing as they fought against enemies on both sides of the Atlantic – royalist Episcopalians, Scottish Presbyterians, Irish Catholics, and Native Americans. Would the theology of killing a pagan in New England differ from that of killing a Presbyterian north of the Tweed?

Military historians often overlook theology and theologians often overlook warfare. In order to understand wartime theology, I examined five decisive victories: the Mystic Massacre (1637), Battle of Naseby (1645), siege of Drogheda (1649), Battle of Dunbar (1650), and the Great Swamp Fight (1675). After each event, partisans made hundreds – sometimes thousands – of theological or scriptural claims. The expressed theology varied, and rival interpretations of victory sprung radially from the events like spokes from a wheel. Beliefs about God's involvement in these events were dynamic and richly textured.

In 1620 Protestants who believed godliness required separation from the Church of England fled and formed a colony in Plymouth. They left Britain due to increasingly coercive measures against religious minorities. Once in New England, there was episodic violence with

---

1. See Matthew Rowley, 'Godly Violence: Military Providentialism in the Puritan Atlantic World, 1636–1676', Ph.D. thesis (University of Leicester, 2018).

Algonquian tribes. This Anglo-Indian relationship, however, was relatively peaceful until the 1670s.

A decade after Plymouth, the Puritans who founded Massachusetts Bay likewise valued peaceful coexistence. Massachusetts, however, rapidly expanded. New settlements in Connecticut afforded more opportunities for conflict with the Pequot tribe. After the death of a notoriously unethical Englishman, the tribe harboured the suspected Pequot murderers – although the Pequot tried to make restitution through other means. This evidences two different legal cultures that spoke past each other on issues of life and death. Miscommunications fed heightened demands for justice that were soon accompanied by escalating violence. Pequot noncompliance convinced the godly that the whole tribe must be held accountable. By 1637, godly forces nearly exterminated this powerful tribe. In the name of valuing life and legal order, Pequot men, women, and children were targeted at their Mystic settlement. The godly then monetised the lethal hunting of humans and executed or enslaved those they captured. Native American slavery became entwined with the importation of enslaved persons from Africa. Theological interpretations of these events were arresting. They danced from godly accounts of war like flames from the inferno at Mystic. As one prominent New England minister remarked, this was 'divine slaughter by the hand of the English'.[2]

As the Pequot War closed, the British Civil Wars opened. The Bishops' Wars with Scotland (1639–1640) were followed by the Irish Rebellion (1641). Finally, England split between royalists and parliamentarians (Charles I raised his standard in 1642). The king's various subjects – for their own reasons – worried about his coercive government that was increasingly seen as arbitrary, unaccountable, and not willing to listen to grievances. As recently argued in *Hot Protestants* by Michael Winship,

> 'puritans on both sides of the Atlantic grappl[ed] with a daunting question throughout this period: how to respond when your monarch or other authorities make a demand of you that you believe violates the laws of

---

2. Thomas Shepard, 'Autobiography', in M. McGiffert (ed.), *God's Plot: Puritan Spirituality in Thomas Shepard's Cambridge* (Amherst: University of Massachusetts Press, 1994), 69.

England and/or God – with defiance, compliance, subterfuge, martyrdom, or even rebellion?'[3]

The godly course of action was far from obvious. Many charged the king with altering church and state. Scripture afforded examples of both sanctified rebellion and patient submission. The godly strained to ensure that their raised sword was not pointed at God and his anointed.

After the battle of Naseby in 1645, the godly hoped providence was driving them towards victory. They produced jubilant accounts of the battle. Many parliamentarian accounts emphasised divine agency, miracles, and the physical non-existence of their forces. Generally speaking, the godly were cautious about supernatural claims, believing them a relic of Catholic superstition. However, they featured prominently in war. The charge of rebellion – coupled with the fact that Charles was personally endangered at Naseby – may have increased supernatural claims. If God himself fought, who could fault his human instruments? The victory mirrored spectacular passages in the Hebrew Bible (particularly the Exodus), and the godly also made arguments related to prodigious events, astrology, eschatology, and prophecy. The battle ended with the slaughter and mutilation of hundreds of women.[4] For various reasons, massacres occurred with greater regularity after a decisive *victory* – and this was true for both Presbyterian and Independent Puritan armies.[5] Godly chroniclers recounted this slaughter of women at Naseby. None showed remorse. Some accounts bordered on glee. When the godly later searched their hearts for 'provoking sins' that led to the loss of power, none (to my knowledge) concluded that this slaughter of women might have provoked God.

In 1649, the godly secured their power by slaying their prince. These were heady days for Independent Puritans. Military plans were often infused with confident eschatological expectancy. Many saw prophetic

3. Michael P. Winship, *Hot Protestants: A History of Puritanism in England and America* (London: Yale University Press, 2019), 4–5.
4. Frank Tallett, 'Barbarism in War: Soldiers and Civilians in the British Isles, c.1641–1652', in George Kassimeris (ed.), *Warrior's Dishonour: Barbarity, Morality and Torture in Modern Warfare* (London, 2006), 29–30.
5. Will Coster, 'Massacre and Codes of Conduct in the English Civil War', in Mark Levene and Penny Roberts (eds), *The Massacre in History* (Oxford, 1999), 94–100.

fulfilment in violent expansion. They prioritised reducing Ireland. Generations of civilising conflict formed layers of sedimented prejudices. These were violently stirred by the Irish Rebellion of 1641. Narratives of Protestants butchered by Catholics – and these accounts were a mixture of truth, exaggeration, and fancy – loomed large in the Puritan mind. In 1649, Oliver Cromwell led a force to Ireland. In the first engagement, he called for the surrender of the Irish Catholic and English royalist defenders of Drogheda. They refused. Irish defenders were guilty of bloodshed since 1641; English defenders of continuing a providentially-damned conflict. This partnership united two streams of bloodguilt in one accursed cause. Sermons after the bloodshed at Drogheda contained some astounding content, printed with the approval of Parliament. One minister encouraged the godly to acclimate to their temporary role as David-like men 'of blood'. How could they be men of peace? '*Jesus Christ* begins now to reign in the Power of his *Death,* as a Man of Blood'.[6] Isaiah's suffering servant became Revelation's slaying saviour, and the godly needed to change vocations with Christ. Bloody were these peacemakers, for they were building God's kingdom on earth. Subduing Scotland came next.

The godly in Scotland and England had much uniting them. The early 1640s saw military cooperation against Charles I and theological cooperation at the Westminster Assembly of Divines. These were Covenanted brethren. Around the time of Naseby, it became evident that faithfulness to God was leading Presbyterians and Independents to advocate different visions of church and state. Conflicts grew among the assembly at Westminster. In the words of Chad Van Dixhoorn:

> 'It was an hour of glory for the puritan experiment.... It has often been said that the godly were unified in times of opposition, but could not survive the experience of power..... [H]owever, the minutes of the assembly suggest that it was not a taste of power that ruined them but the fear that they had so little power at all'.[7]

---

6. Peter Sterry, *The commings forth of Christ in the power of his death* (London, 1649), 11.

7. C. Van Dixhoorn (ed.), *Minutes and Papers of the Westminster Assembly, 1643–52* (Oxford: Oxford University Press, 2012) I:81–82.

Independents often rooted faithfulness in following the ever-moving and unpredictable God. This led them away from their prior support for the Covenant. Presbyterians, by contrast, often defined faithfulness as unswerving commitment to the Covenant. The regicide drove the camps further apart. The Scots' declaration of Charles II over all the British Isles was interpreted as aggressive. The godly in England felt compelled to act. Brothers in Christ fought like siblings – their similarities fuelled an unguarded contempt.

At Dunbar in 1650, the dejected and outnumbered parliamentarians defeated the powerful and confident Covenanters – tempering Presbyterian political optimism and supernaturalism. But how could it be holy or just to kill a brother in Christ? As for justice, the Independents felt compelled to fight a foe bent on imposing civil and religious systems on England. As for holiness, there was a thin line between communion and conflict, particularly when partners in a holy cause became obstacles. Independent ministers levied all of Scripture against Scotland. Covenanters were called Pharaoh, Balaam, Dagon, Amalekites, Sodomites, and whores. They were tarred with terms like herem and anathema.[8] The Scottish were 'vipers, serpents, wolves'. Although they looked like saints, some were 'a devil incarnate'.[9] Although the godly might want to show mercy to their *brothers*, one minister pressed home the example of the God-ordained slaughter of Benjaminite *brethren* (Judges 20).[10] The Scots were Covenanters *and* Canaanites.[11] The Covenant was 'an *Achan* in the *Scots Army*',[12] and the godly stoned it at Dunbar.

With the British Isles pacified, the godly broadened their horizons. They were soon at war with the Dutch, followed by war with Spain. Some hoped to march on Rome. Fortuna was fickle, and power slipped

---

8. These were some of the harshest terms in scripture, hurled against Israel's enemies (herem) and against those who perverted the gospel (anathema).
9. Thomas Brooks, *The hypocrite detected, anatomized, impeached, arraigned, and condemned before the Parliament of England* (London, 1650), 1–6.
10. Nathaniel Homes, *A sermon, preached before the Right Honourable, Thomas Foote* (London, 1650).
11. E.g. John Canne, *Emanuel, or, God with us* (London, 1650), 19–27.
12. Ibid., 19–20.

through their palms. 'Puritanism' in the words of John Morrill, 'both triumphed and disintegrated in the English Revolution'.[13]

This disintegration paved the way for the Restoration of the Stuarts. Godly societies then became a scarce resource, increasing the value of New England.

Before the Pequot War, Puritans could only dream of power in England. By the time of King Philip's War in the 1670s, that dream was a memory. In 1675, Plymouth executed three members of the Wampanoag tribe for a murder. Many elements of the trial were suspect, exacerbating decades-old tensions. As the region plunged into violence, the godly felt they were experiencing covenantal curses. The scale of violence was unprecedented for New England – leading to the fragmentation of civil and (especially) religious authority. Christian Indians were singled out for especially harsh policies and mob attacks – and they were quarantined on an island in the dead of winter. A conspiracy to slaughter these Christians was narrowly thwarted. As the war deepened, the godly were willing to try something – almost anything – to avert God's wrath. They could not get their enemies to beat scalping knives into pruning hooks. Military failure led to experimental piety. In an attempt to turn the tide of the war, they attacked a neutral tribe, the Narragansett, at the Great Swamp. The slaughter was great but the victory was pyrrhic. Although God granted victory, they thought it was given 'by terrible things in righteousness'.[14] King Philip's War devastated the region (especially for the Algonquian tribes). The godly were so weakened that the Stuarts finally subjected the colonies. The age of autonomous Puritan politics was over.

Puritan theology predated political puritanism, and their theology lived on long after political puritanism was forced to an end. In Old and New England, there was a different process whereby Puritans gained and lost power. These differences impacted the centuries-long influence in each

---

13. John Morrill, 'The Puritan Revolution', in John Coffey and Paul C. H. Lim (eds), *The Cambridge Companion to Puritanism* (Cambridge: Cambridge University Press, 2008), 84.

14. J. Hammond Trumbull (ed.), *Journal of the Council of War, 1675 to 1678*, 408. Found in volume two of J. Hammond Trumbull, et al. (eds), *The Public Records of the Colony of Connecticut, 1636–1665*, 15 vols. (Hartford, 1850–1890).

region, as noted by Mark Noll.[15] In Britain, Puritans were viewed as righteously zealous in an unjust cause. They were, therefore, not to be trusted with power. Eventually, a modified Puritan temperament reemerged in the progressive party in British politics.

The story was different in New England. Even though the godly lost autonomy in the wake of King Philip's War, their dominance over Native Americans increased. By the time the American Revolution restored autonomy to the colonies, New England had moved on from exclusive political puritanism. The conviction that providence placed the English over Native Americans was durable and diverse. This song of superiority could be sung to different tunes, depending on the occasion: American Revolution, Manifest Destiny, international interventionism, scientific racism and determinism, benevolent assimilation, economic affluence, victory in the World Wars, and continued dominance in foreign relations. Each occasion influenced how Americans remembered colonial warfare.

---

15. Mark Noll, *In the Beginning Was the Word: The Bible in American Public Life, 1492–1783* (Oxford, 2016), 15, 72–74, 83.

Protestants elevated the written word. Scripture was foremost, but they also greatly valued catechisms, confessions, theological treatises, and the printed sermon. It is important that we not overemphasise these documents as we attempt to understand lived theology. As cautioned by Alec Ryrie, it is easy to forget that 'Christians are more than credal statements on legs'.[1] This is especially true when beliefs were refracted through the prism of politics.

Some, doubtless, manipulated Scripture like a wax nose.[2] It was more often the case that individuals approached Scripture, genuinely seeing their politics flow from the text. As helpfully worded by Kevin Killeen, 'The verses were, in their way, a Rorschach test – the political psychology of the observer emerging in how they responded to the text'.[3] Scripture required an interpreter – interpreters were temperamentally diverse and historically rooted. It is little wonder, then, that politics and war influenced interpretations.

The thirst for power changed Puritan theology, often in ways that went unnoticed. There were general patterns, detailed below, that emerge from the rise and decline of political puritanism. Each of these discussions deserve more attention and nuance than is given here.

Prejudice and Providence

The *Oxford English Dictionary* lists several 'obsolete' definitions of prejudice:

> '[1] The action of judging an event beforehand; prognostication, presaging. [2] A prior judgement; esp. a judgement formed hastily or before due consideration. [3] A preliminary or anticipatory judgement; a

---

1. Alec Ryrie, *Being Protestant in Reformation Britain* (Oxford: Oxford University Press, 2013), 1.
2. The phrase is from Erasmus (B. Radice [trans.] and A.H.T. Levi [ed.], *Desiderius Erasmus: Praise of Folly* [Repr.; London: Penguin, 1993], 94).
3. Kevin Killeen, *The Political Bible in Early Modern England* (Cambridge: Cambridge University Press, 2017), 128.

preconceived idea as to what will happen; an anticipation'.

It is in these senses that providence was closely related to prejudice.

Relating providence to prejudice might seem counterintuitive since the doctrine is fundamentally about God, not prejudice-prone humans. However, it is people who claim to perceive particular providences; who attach meanings to events.

Providentialism could be deeply partisan. David Hume, unsurprisingly, looked askance at the practice. He noted how the godly drew 'forced inferences' from events. Believers interpreted events 'as a confirmation of their particular prejudices'.[4] One commentator who lived through the Civil Wars succinctly worded this point: 'construction follows opposition'.[5] One constructed a providential narrative around what they opposed. This might be represented as follows:

> If I am opposed to X political position, then I will interpret event A as confirmation that God likewise opposes X.

Of course, the believer would not think this represented their procession of thoughts. They might say:

> Since God opposed X political position, and since the Holy Spirit led me to oppose X, it should be expected that event A confirms that X was wrong.

Modern theorists might call this 'confirmation bias'; early modern Christians might have considered it faithful living.

It was easy to challenge the partisan providentialism of opponents, but the godly had a harder time recognising their own prejudices. Sir Archibald Johnston of Wariston was a particularly influential Scotsman. He, along with the minister Alexander Henderson, drafted the Scottish National Covenant (1638). His providentialism was of the Presbyterian-

---

4. David Hume, *The history of Great Britain. Containing the common wealth, and part of the reign of Charles II* (Dublin, 1757) III:137.
5. Edward Gee, *A treatise of prayer and of divine providence* (London, 1653), 216.

confirming variety. In a sober diary entry he reflected on providential manipulation:

> 'I thought I was following the call of Gods providence...
> the trueth is I followed the call of providence when it
> agreed with my humour and pleased my idol and
> seemed to tend to honor and advantage'.[6]

God's voice penetrating through the darkness was sometimes the sound of his own desires echoing off the back of the cave.

Providence was a powerful and all-encompassing doctrine that had the advantage of forceful simplicity. However, a causal theory that explained everything, in general, ran the risk of explaining nothing in particular.[7] Opponents agreed God providentially brought about all things, including event A. But why did God bring about event A and not event B? Puritans and their opponents fought over the *particulars*. The more details people tacked on to the doctrine, the more it could be used to attack opponents. This was particularly true of providential 'because' and 'therefore' statements. 'Because we did X, God brought about event A. Therefore we should now do Z'. One entered murky waters when they used providence to chart practice, as several prominent ministers warned.[8]

Partisans turned to Scripture to settle providential debates, but Scripture's manifold witness proved elastic and uncontrollable. Scriptural complexity rendered the debates intractable. Partisans found at least four ways of interpreting judgements and four of interpreting mercies. Were *judgements* the result (1) of something believers did right (a test of faith);[9] (2) a chastisement for sin;[10] (3) the by-product of an

---

6. Archibald Johnston, *Diary of Sir Archibald Johnston of Wariston*, G. M. Paul et al. (eds.), (Edinburgh: Scottish History Society, 1940) III:167.

7. A similar point is made in Carl Trueman, *Histories and Fallacies: Problems Faced in the Writing of History* (Wheaton: Crossway, 2010), 166–67.

8. John Calvin, *Institutes of the Christian Religion*, trans. Henry Beveridge (Peabody: Hendrickson, 2008) I.17.3–5; John Flavel, *The mystery of Providence* (London, 1678), *Works* IV:469; John Warren, *The potent potter* (London, 1649), 14; Thomas Watson, *A body of practical divinity* (London, 1692), 71.

9. Job 1:1–2:10; Matt 5:10–12; John 15:18; 2 Tim 3:12; 1 Pet 2:19–20; 3:14; 4:14, 16; 1 John 3:13.

10. Lev 26:14–46; Num 16:22; Deut 4:25–28; 28:15–68; Josh 7; 2 Sam 24:17.

outsider's sin;[11] (4) or were the grounds for God's judgements shrouded in mystery?[12] Were *mercies* the result of (a) something believers did right;[13] (b) a gracious act even though they did something wrong;[14] (c) the by-product of an outsider's sin;[15] (d) or were the causes of God's blessings mysterious?[16] Who decided which scriptural precedent applied to event A? This brief sketch was only the tip of the iceberg of providential complexity and elasticity, and I provide much more detail and nuance elsewhere.[17]

The manifold witness of Scripture accounted for much of the variations in providential discourse. It made it difficult to authoritatively map verses onto a given situation. Individual Puritans, and godly communities writ large wrote about providence differently depending on circumstances. David Fergusson recently argued that different types of providential beliefs cohabitate in a single mind:

> 'Many of us probably live according to some theology of providence, at least an inchoate or implicit one. Indeed, we may have several theologies of providence inside our heads, our particular moods and circumstances determining which of these is dominant at any one time'.[18]

He rightly notes how war is one of the primary causes of mental shifts between various understandings of providence.

Victory or defeat, success or failure, want or plenty, peace or war – all could be taken as evidence that one had a righteous cause. As conflicts dragged on, Puritans doubled their efforts to use providence to convince enemies. They sowed bold declarations about providence in the rocky soil of disbelief. In the long run, they seemed to have reaped doubt. For

---

11. Josh 7; 1 Pet 2:19–20; 2 Pet 2:6–8.
12. Deut 29:29; Ecc 9:11; Amos 3:6; Isa 45:7; Lam 3:38; Luke 13:3–5; John 9:1–5; Rom 11:33.
13. Lev 26:1–13; Deut 4:29–31; 28:1–14; 30:1–10; 2 Chron 20:20.
14. Rom 2:4; 2 Pet 3:9.
15. Deut 9:5; Rom 11:11–12.
16. Deut 29:29; Ecc 9:11; Matt 5:45; Rom 11:33.
17. Rowley, 'Godly Violence', 187–202.
18. David Fergusson, *The Providence of God: A Polyphonic Approach* (Cambridge: Cambridge University Press, 2018), 3.

example, Deism grew in popularity *after* the wars of religion. It followed the incessant use of providence to justify politics. Deism, in part, followed political providentialism. Martyn Cowan noted this in his 2016 St Antholin's Lecture: 'Undoubtably, the hubris that marked the interpretation of providence by Owen and others like him was a factor that promoted the process of decline' in beliefs about God's involvement in history.[19] Weaponising providence for political and military ends seldom convinced outsiders and jeopardised the credibility of the doctrine.

Leading God Into War

The godly – and those they opposed – lived through very trying times. The political and religious situations in the British Isles and colonial New England seemed uncertain and perhaps unprecedented. It was unfamiliar terrain for all involved. The godly, in general, looked at various maps to chart their course – the laws of God, of nations, and of England. They also looked to the compass of conscience. Even with these various resources – or perhaps because these resources varied – the correct path was often not well marked. Added to this, the civil and religious guides often pointed the faithful towards opposite political positions. One leader's clear command from Scripture was another's unclear precedent – and vice versa.

The godly still needed to act: submit or rebel; fight or flee; justify war or critique it? As decisions become more controversial, the godly increasingly attributed their beliefs and actions to the will, leading or agency of God. Just as Thomas Hobbes simplified the issue of authority by positing an overarching *Leviathan*, so appeals to God's will, agency, and leading could simplify the Christian's decision-making process.

Ministers often agonised over supporting a cause, knowing their assent was in- valuable. However, approval of a cause was like the endorsement of a controversial politician—no matter how hedged the endorsement, proponents of the cause/candidate will only remember the affirmation. If a tepid 'Yes' is placed on top a wall of 'Noes', many people will only see the elevated 'Yes'. Erasmus noted this when writing of the early

---

19. Martyn C. Cowan, *Portrait of a Prophet: Lessons from the Preaching of John Owen (1616–1683)* (London: Latimer Trust, 2016), 32.

church fathers on killing: They 'approved of war in one or two passages', but 'how many passages are there where they condemn and curse it?'.[20] Christians ran with Augustine's 'Yes' and forgot his many 'Noes'.

When controversial decisions were attributed to God, some of the burden of responsibility could be shifted from humans. To some extent, the more controversial a decision, the higher the risk is that the decision was ethically questionable. This, perhaps, is why controversial decisions were often attributed to the leading or agency of God *alone*. This might sound counterintuitive, but it was also perfectly understandable. One might think that the more controversial – and thus uncertain – a decision was, the less the god-fearing partisan might want to involve God in it. The opposite was often the case. For example, when fighting against the king at Naseby, some Puritan ministers spoke of their armies as if they were non-existent. God alone fought and secured the victory. In this war, they frequently said there was little of man in the event and much of God. When they eventually executed the king, it was the leading of God that brought them to it.

Relatedly, attributing human activity to God could lead to a downplaying of the lingering depravity among the redeemed. They might also background the common grace given to their enemies. In complex ways, using a variety of doctrines and scriptural texts, many Puritans attributed their most controversial actions and decisions to the leading and agency of God.

In the late 1640s and 1650s, many felt hitched to providence and pulled towards wars in Ireland and Scotland and also against the Dutch and Spanish. They were willing to fight wherever providence pulled them. Although many claimed there was no 'admixture' of man in their decisions, to an outsider, their thought-processes appear human, all too human.

Glorifying the God of Battles

Even though the New Testament said to glorify God in *all things* (I Cor 10:31), Christians also held that *some things* should not be done to the glory of God – precisely because these things should not be done. This

---

20. Lisa Jardin (ed), *Erasmus: The Education of a Christian Prince* (Cambridge: Cambridge University Press, 1997), 105.

was a subtle distinction with enormous implications for war. The desire to glorify God often restricted the actions of the godly, particularly because they did not want to dishonour God. Dedicating unjust actions to God would only increase guilt. The desire to do everything to the glory of God often increased justice and made persons more merciful and humane. However, the need to glorify God could also loose people from ordinary standards of justice and allow them to be ruthless warriors.

Victory, writ large, benefited the godly, and it is understandable why ministers thanked God for it. Their aim in war was often not selfish aggrandisement but the protection of the vulnerable and the safeguarding of civil and religious rights. The godly, however, thanked God for the outcome of war and for the messy details of combat. Apparently with a clean conscience, many glorified God for his part in the more controversial aspects of these campaigns. Those wars involved the killing of soldiers and civilians. The conflicts detailed above featured slavery, stripping women civilians, shooting sleeping civilians, executing female camp followers, separating Native American children from their parents, breaking treaties, forging documents, mutilating women, etc. These things should not have been done to the glory of God precisely because they should not have been done.

The Cannon and the Canon

When Christians entered the political and martial spheres, they often did so with a pared down version of Scripture. There was, in other words, a functional canon within the canon. Most notably, the Hebrew Bible dominated wartime theology. The godly relied heavily on passages about destruction and deliverance – particularly the exodus, wilderness, conquest, and the period of the judges. Many believed themselves to be in some form of a covenantal relationship with God akin to ancient Israel. They even adopted themes of works righteousness when it came to corporate matters.[21] Some went so far as to use Catholic sacramental language to describe war.[22] Of the 217 sermons delivered to Parliament

---

21. Harry S. Stout, *New England Soul: Preaching and Religious Culture in Colonial New England* (Repr.; Oxford, 2012), 27.
22. Susan Juster, *Sacred Violence in Early America* (Philadelphia, 2016), 53; cf. 17–75.

during the Civil Wars, 162 came from the Hebrew Bible and 14 from Revelation. Of the 41 remaining, ministers took the text from less than half of the books of the New Testament.[23]

The Hebrew Bible was filled with stories that could be related to later conflicts: accounts of kings and conquests, submissions and rebellions, false and faithful prophets. Political typology proved as alluring as it was uncontrollable. There were, in essence, too many types in Scripture. There were too many (good or bad) kings, subjects or foreign nations – and no one in early modern England had the authority to decide which applied in their present situation. The Puritans amassed 'types' and stoned their enemies with them; opponents simply picked them up and threw them back.

Many also invoked the sacrificial system in creative ways. For example, John Owen mixed a cocktail of ritual sacrifice and eschatology, serving it to an audience eager to understand the defeat of Scottish Presbyterian and royalist Episcopalians.

> That blood which is an acceptable sacrifice to the Lord, is the blood of the enemies of this designe of his [i.e. of building a holy temple on earth]: the vengeance that is to be delighted in, is the *Vengeance of the Temple:* Heaven and all that is in it, is called to rejoyce, when *Babylon is destroyed with violence and fury, Rev.* 18.20, 21. when those who would not have the King of Saints reigne, are brought forth and slaine before his face: and in this, God makes distinguishing worke, and calls to rejoycing.... Thus the Saints are called to sing the *song of Moses the servant of God* ['Temporall deliverance'], *and the song of the Lamb* ['spirituall deliverance'].[24]

---

23. John F. Wilson, *Pulpit in Parliament: Puritanism During the English Civil Wars, 1640–1648* (Princeton: Princeton University Press, 1968), 146–55.
24. John Owen, *The advantage of the kingdome of Christ in the shaking of the kingdoms of the world* (Oxford: 1651), 16–17.

Although Owen wrote against the practice of human sacrifice,[25] this passage about rejoicing over the deaths of enemies is arresting.

The uses of the Psalter are also important. David modelled passionate leadership, ruthless piety, single-minded devotion, and merciful restraint. Through certain Psalms, some gave full vent to a jubilant hatred of enemies. The vengeance of David may have allowed them to bypass New Testament commands about loving enemies. A poem by William Barton after the Independent victory over Scottish Presbyterians at Dunbar illustrates this:

> 'I have pursu'd our foes that fled,
>   and also overta'ne,
> And till they were extinguished
>   I did not turn again [Ps 18:37].
> They had not strength enough to rise,
>   I wounded them so sore;
> Beneath my feet mine Enemies
>   are faln in bloody gore [Ps 18:38]....
> Mine Enemies necks into my hand,
>   are given me by thee,
> That I might root out of the Land
>   all them that hated me [Ps 18:40]....
> As small as dust that's blown about
>   when boysterous winds do meet,
> I beat my foes, and cast them out
>   as dirt into the street [Ps 18:42]'.[26]

This work was approved for publication by a former Westminster divine.

The book of Jeremiah was also important because the prophet warned of covenantal curses if God's people did not repent. He called the faithful back to the covenant. Like Israel, the godly were victimised by their

---

25. 'Hinc ad infandum, horrendum, detestandum illud *facinus* (Ἀνθρωποθυσίασ scilicet)' (J. Owen, *Diatriba de justitia divina* [Oxford, 1653], 67).
26. William Barton, *Hallelujah. Or certain hymns, composed out of Scripture, to celebrate some special and publick occasions* (London, 1651), 36–37. This publication repurposed an earlier poem for Dunbar.

enemies – and this was the result of sin against God. Adrian Weimer refers to something similar as the blending of 'martyrdom themes' with 'jeremiad themes'.[27] Especially in war against Native Americans, the godly stressed that they sinned against God and their English neighbours. They rarely considered that they might have sinned against the Native Americans. It is not surprising, then, that few comprehended why their Algonquian enemies were so angry. This raises the intriguing possibility that, sometimes, there might be a correlation between introspection and the denial of guilt.

Whole portions of the New Testament seemed to temporarily vanish during conflict. For example, during King Philip's War, prayers were frequently made for their enemies destruction. Under the strain of war – and doubtless in response to the loss of loved ones – few offered prayers *for their enemies* (Matt 5:43–44). As another example, when Colonel John Hewson used spiritual eyes to describe the conquest of Drogheda, he relied entirely on the Hebrew Bible (save a brief excursion into Revelation). Drogheda's defenders became Israel's enemies.[28] Similarly, a chaplain for the kirk's forces fed the troops on a narrow slice of Scripture (his diary records eleven sermons on the Hebrew Bible for every one on the New Testament). He spent considerable time taking the troops through the imprecations in Psalm 83. His few sermons from the New Testament were directed at political ends.[29]

Many inhabited the Hebrew Bible eschatologically. The books of Daniel and Revelation were also important in war. Eschatological beliefs defy the neat categorisation found in systematic theologies – particularly because expectations rose and fell in tandem with political success. As was shown above, inhabiting the past (e.g. the exodus or conquest) helped the godly understand their present. They also turned to the biblical future and found themselves written into the narratives. Eschatology rose in prominence because of the works of Thomas Brightman (1562–1607), Joseph Mede (1586–1638) and John Cotton

---

27. Adrian Chastain Weimer, *Martyr's Mirror: Persecution and Holiness in Early New England* (Oxford: Oxford University Press, 2011), 126.

28. Richard Collings (ed.), *The kingdomes weekly intelligencer* (2nd–9th Oct 1649) Issue 332: 1522, 1524.

29. Robert Douglas, 'Mr. Robert Douglas's Diary, 1644', in James Burns, *Memoirs by James Burns, Bailie of the City of Glasgow, 1644–1661* (Edinburgh, 1832), 51–80.

(1585–1652), among many others. During the Civil Wars, frequent and intense speculations flourished – particularly among the Independents. The Fifth Monarchy Men, though far from mainstream, were symptomatic of the times. Changing eschatological beliefs are noticeable in comments on war. For example, partisans fighting the Pequot seldom invoked Daniel or Revelation. These portions of Scripture grew in importance by the time of Naseby and featured prominently in interpretations of Drogheda and Dunbar. The Restoration in England, and King Philip's War in New England stripped the godly of much of their eschatological confidence.

There were also dangers in the ever-expanding definitions of the Antichrist. The term became so elastic that, for some Independent Puritans, that even Scottish Presbyterians were in league with him. There was the Antichrist (person #1), people supporting the Antichrist directly (persons #2), people supporting the supporters (persons #3). Nathaniel Homes made this clear in a sermon. Over the decade, lowlander Presbyterians came to 'uphold the present Kings of the earth', and thus to 'uphold the *upholders of Antichrist*'. This is why 'those that uphold such upholders, must fall'.[30]

More than Conquerors Through Christ

Many Puritans – from lay members to revered divines – seem to have forgotten Christ crucified when they were put into political situations (although they emphasised Revelation's conqueror). The Gospels and the person and work of Christ are seldom mentioned. Since the New Testament was written to marginalised and persecuted Christians who *were not* seeking political power, most of the New Testament sits awkwardly with political puritanism. Below are a few examples of how Christ could be backgrounded.

During England's political transition, John Owen Owen wrote at length on the person and work of Christ. For example, he composed *Of the death of Christ, the price he paid, and the purchase he made* (1650) while accompanying the army in the con- quest of Ireland. He dedicated it to Oliver Cromwell – who by the time of publication was already

---

30. Nathaniel Homes, *A sermon, preached before the Right Honourable, Thomas Foote* (London, 1650), 39.

accused of butchery. In his political sermons, he drew mainly on the Hebrew Bible: *Eben-ezer a memoriall of the deliverance of Essex* (1648) [Hab 3:1–9]; *A sermon preached to the Honourable House of Commons* (1649) [Jer 15:19–20]; Ουρανων ουρανια, *the shaking and translating of heaven and earth* (1649) [Heb 12:27]; *The branch of the Lord, the beauty of Sion* (1650) [Isa 56:7]; *The stedfastness of promises, and the sinfulness of staggering* (1650) [Rom 4:20]; *The advantage of the kingdome of Christ in the shaking of the kingdoms of the world* (1651) [Ezek 17:24]; *The labouring saints dismission to rest* (1652) [Dan 12:13]; *A sermon preached to the Parliament* (1652) [Dan 7:15–16]. Three things should be mentioned. First, it is difficult to tell the content from the sermon text and titles. Many of these sermons contain deep reflections on Jesus, and Owen was adept at seeing Christ in the Hebrew Bible. However, the choice of sermon text reveals something about his scriptural orientation. Second, Owen preached two sermons from the New Testament: the Hebrews sermon emphasised es- chatological fulfilment; the Romans one challenged Parliament with Abraham's faithful- ness. Third, these sermons often portray Christ as one tearing down an enemy kingdom or building up his own (through godly instruments).

Another example comes from a widely distributed catechism from the Civil Wars. Parliament issued *The souldiers pocket Bible* in 1643. The Scriptures – in their entirety – would be cumbersome to carry and expensive to produce. Instead, soldiers were given select verses intended to 'supply the want of the whole Bible'. The catechism relied, almost entirely, on the Hebrew Bible. Moses featured prominently, but Jesus was absent. When Christian soldiers went into battle, their pocket Bibles left Jesus out. Even on flags carried into battle, mottoes from the Hebrew Bible outnumbered ones from the New Testament two to one.[31]

Similarly, one of the most important works from Puritan New England, Mary Rowlandson's captivity narrative, relied almost entirely on the covenantal relationship between God and Israel to explain her capture and redemption.[32] She nowhere wrote of the Holy Spirit, Messiah,

---

31. Ian Gentles, 'The Iconography of Revolution: 1642–1649', in Ian Gentles, John Morrill and Blair Worden (eds), *Soldiers, Writers and Statesmen of the English Revolution* (Cambridge, 1998), 98.
32. Mary Rowlandson, *The soveraignty & goodness of God* (Cambridge, 1682).

Savior, Jesus or Christ. Moses convicted her of sin. Israel's covenant illumined the road to redemption. Jesus played no part in the narrative she told.

As quoted earlier, Christopher Hitchens wrote of the 'very intoxicating' feeling of being 'yoked to the great steam engine of history'. One Puritan came to believe that union with Christ allowed the godly to *operate* the steam engine (or I should say '*Ship*'). The godly were 'One' with Christ and acted in accord with him, Peter Sterry argued in 1649. He then mixed a unique blend of theology and politics:

> 'The whole *Creation* is, a *Ship. God* is the *Pilot. Jesus Christ* is the *Helme,* by which *God* governes, and turnes about the World. A Saint is *One Piece* with *Christ* in the *Helm.* He hath his *Hand* with the Father upon this Helme. Thus he rules in the World, sitting at the Helm of things in the *Lap* of his Father, and growing into One Helme, or Rudder with Christ by His Embraces. *All things are Yours, and You are Christs, and Christ is Gods,* 1 Cor. 3'.[33]

Although his language was opaque, it is clear he was talking about three persons: the first two members of the Godhead and the Christian. The unity of the Christian with Christ was so complete that believers could steer the ship of creation. The will of God collapsed into the will of the godly – although they might have seen the collapse as going the other way. Parliament asked that this sermon be printed for public consumption.

For some Christians, the experience of victimisation seemed to anchor them to the experience of Christ – who never resorted to the sword. Roger Williams experienced what he identified as wrongs throughout his life – exile from the Puritan colonies ranking foremost among them. He, like his Puritan neighbours, supported war when he thought the cause was just. However, his writings on war were notable because he tried to lead the godly towards mercy by reminding them of the *crucified* Christ. They forgot Christ in conflict, he thought, because they privileged the Hebrew Bible. His coreligionists were 'preferring of

---

33. Peter Sterry, *The commings forth of Christ in the power of his death* (London, 1649), 22.

Moses the Servant, before the *Lord Jesus* the Son, yea and (consequently) a denying of the *Lord Jesus*, the great Messiah, to be yet come?'[34] The godly, he charged, acted as if the incarnation were reversed.

Williams' reflections remained anchored in the person and work of Christ, and this had important implications for his views of conscience, toleration, and the relationship between church and state. When the godly opened the door to persecuting dissenters, he wrote in a letter, they will eventually have 'persecuted *Jesus* in some of them'. He continued: 'I must be humbly bold to say, that 'tis impossible for any Man or Men to maintaine their *Christ* by the *Sword*, and to worship a true *Christ* to fight against all *Consciences* opposite to theirs, and not to fight against *God* in some of them'.[35] Out of love for Christ in the Christian, Williams implored toleration.[36]

Pardon before Prosecution

Puritan ministers often counselled forgiveness and forbearance in response to wrongs suffered. Although the experience of *personal* victimisation could be intoxicating, individuals often refused the cup. Many times, the reaction was different when the wrongs were against the group, particularly when there were obligations to protect the innocent and prosecute the guilty. Here the Christian call to suffer for Christ came into friction with other duties. In the novel *Gilead*, Marilynne Robinson included a similar tension in a letter from an ageing minister to his young son:

> 'Harm to you is not harm to me in the strict sense, and that is a great part of the problem. He could knock me down the stairs and I would have worked out the theology for forgiving him before I reached the bottom.

---

34. Roger Williams, *The Examiner Defended* (1652) *Works* VII:262
35. 'Roger Williams to John Endicott' (Aug-Sept 1651) in Glenn W. LaFantasie (ed.), *The Correspondence of Roger Williams* (London: Brown University Press, 1988) I:337–51.
36. For more on his thought, see Matthew Rowley, '"All Pretend an Holy War": Radical Beliefs and the Rejection of Persecution in the Mind of Roger Williams', *The Review of Faith & International Affairs*, 15, no. 2 (2017), 66–76.

But if he hurt you in the slightest way, I'm afraid theology would fail me'.[37]

When *personally* wronged, godly ministers frequently decried vengeance and encouraged forgiveness, forbearance, and love of enemies. When the wrong was corporate or political, the response often differed.

Much of the driving force behind political puritanism was the desire to redress grievances and prevent them from reoccurring. Whether the injustices were legal innovation, an arbitrary and unaccountable monarch, or the slaughter of Protestants in Catholic-majority countries, the godly felt called to action.

It was often victimisation that sent the godly searching for remedies in the Hebrew Bible, and they often had good reasons to think that they were victims. However, they could be blind to how they had victimised others. Ambiguities like this are difficult to grapple with, as noted by Diane Enns in *The Violence of Victimhood*:

> 'What we don't know is how to deal with the messy moral and political quandaries caused by the violent actions of victims. When the line between guilt and innocence wavers, when we are not sure who is responsible for what, and when we are overwhelmed by compassion or pity for the victim who victimizes, we can become unsettled by the ambiguity of events and our resulting ambivalence'.[38]

The currency of conflict often depicts the same face on both sides of the coin – the victimised on one side was often the victimiser on the other. This suggests hidden dangers in a just cause, namely to redress wrongs through force puts one on a slippery slope that could lead to the creation of new victims.

The Puritans were keenly aware of injustice, and they wanted to do something about it. But how did these victims come to victimise? There were, of course, many different paths that led to the same destination –

---

37. Marilynne Robinson, *Gilead* (Repr.; London: Virago, 2005), 217.
38. Diane Enns, *The Violence of Victimhood* (University Park: The Pennsylvania State University Press, 2012), 1.

including the well-worn shortcut from injustice to retaliation. I am more interested in the circuitous route.

Christian beliefs increased the criteria for how believers should respond to those who wronged them. The New Testament exerted significant pressure on the Christian, pushing them towards forgiveness, mercy, and reconciliation. At the same time, it discouraged vengeance. The state, however, was entrusted with the sword, and this opened up the possibility for direct Christian involvement in retribution. However, the pressure towards mercy was still there.

Christians, I am suggesting, were like a coiled spring.[39] When wronged, Scripture helped them absorb wrongs. The coil tightened. Further wrongs presented more opportunities to forgive and show mercy – hoping the opponent would repent. The coil tightened further. There was, however, a point where the tension became unbearable – and that threshold would have differed between persons and groups. Often there was a growing sense that continued mercy would facilitate injustice, leaving innocent persons vulnerable. The coil then released its built-up energy. The patience, mercy, and forgiveness wound into the coil was released onto the offender. Full force went into prosecution with increased vigour and decreased mercy. The built-up energy powered unrelenting justice.[40] A common feature of Puritan warfare – even of battles that ended in massacre – was a deep and abiding sense that the godly had been patient, forgiving, and merciful victims.

Slaying in the Spirit

Spiritual warfare permeated Puritan political thought. Godly ministers produced several large treatises on the topic during times of political upheavals, most notably William Gurnall's, *The Christian in compleat armour* (1655–62). Allegorical works like John Bunyan's *The Pilgrim's*

---

39. I adapt the idea from John Morrill, 'The Nature of the English Revolution', in John Morrill (ed.), *The Nature of the English Revolution: Essays by John Morrill* (London: Longman, 1993), 15.

40. See also Alan Page Fiske and Tage Shakti Rai, *Virtuous Violence: Hurting and Killing to Create, Sustain, End and Honor Social Relationships* (Cambridge: Cambridge University Press, 2015), 4–5, 155, 159.

Progress (1678) and *The Holy War* (1682) fictionalised spiritual struggles and were masterpieces of ecclesiastical *and political* dissent.[41]

Individual soldiers of Christ formed part of a larger force. This 'Church militant' longed for deeper union with Christ, and therefore it 'doth wrastle as yet with enemies in the field of this World', as argued by William Ames.[42] Their way of life was a life of war. In *Violence Victorious* Richard Sibbes advocated the violent pursuit of Christ (Matt 11:12). He was keen to explain what this violence did *not* entail. It could not be 'a violence of iniquity and injustice; and so the people of God, of all others, ought not to be violent people.... Violence rather debars out of the kingdom of heaven than is any qualification for it'.[43] Believers in salvation by faith, the godly also spoke of damnation by works – and unjust killing sufficed to secure a conviction.

Spiritual warfare was generally considered distinct from physical warfare. This did not mean that spiritual soldiery and physical soldiery were incompatible, provided the cause was just. However, political circumstances pressured doctrines of spiritual war. Christians in crisis often face the temptation to harness biblical resources towards ends that sit awkwardly with the original text. The sociologist, David Martin, aptly summarises this:

> 'Christianity turns on the oxymoron, the first being last, the lord being servant, God becoming Man, strength achieved in weakness, and life saved by self-giving. The primary oxymoron is the warfare of the cross and the whole armour of salvation. Christianity captured the language of war for the purpose of peace. But no victory of that kind is fully secure'.[44]

---

41. David Walker, 'Militant religion and politics in *The Holy War*', in Anne Dunan-Page (ed.), *The Cambridge Companion to Bunyan* (Cambridge: Cambridge University Press, 2010), 107-119.
42. William Ames, *The marrow of sacred divinity drawne out of the Holy Scriptures* (London, 1642), 154.
43. Richard Sibbes, *Violence Victorious* (London, 1639), *Works* VI:300; cf. 167, 293-314.
44. David Martin, *Does Christianity Cause War?* (Vancouver, 1997), 112-13.

New Testament writers repurposed the language of war *before* any Christians used physical force to kill; *before* any attempted to build a Christian state with the sword. As Christians thirsted for power, the language of spiritual warfare seemed to satisfy the political need.

Ephesians 6 bifurcated physical violence from spiritual violence, ruling out the former. Yet this passage is frequently quoted in war. Examples like this, in Martin's words, show how 'the symbolic logic of Christianity... is transformed under social pressure'.[45] The meaning behind words and symbols migrates. He notes how this transformation is common in places where 'religion becomes virtually coextensive with society and thus with the dynamics of power, violence, control, cohesion and the marking out of boundaries'.[46]

Spiritual warfare language was often used to promote or baptise war. The *context* and *content* of theological utterances were important. Below I detail four contexts where spiritual warfare bled into physical warfare. First, ministers frequently preached on political occasions or in connection with military events.[47] Hundreds of such sermons exist from the early modern period, most notably the Paul's Cross sermons, the Parliamentary fast and thanksgiving sermons during the Civil Wars, and the artillery and election sermons in England and colonial America. Second, ministers used their platform to influence magistrates, often urging them to execute justice. Thus Thomas Watson's *Heaven taken by storm* (1670) – a work on spiritual violence – was dedicated to the mayor of London who 'bears not the Sword in vain'.[48] Third, political figures may hold religious authority. For example, Charles I's coronation involved three swords: The Sword of Spiritual Justice (obtuse), The Sword of Temporal Justice (pointed), and The Sword of Mercy (blunted).[49] Because the swords were united in one person, it was hard to demarcate the boundaries between them. When Puritans gained power in the British Isles and colonial America, they simultaneously distanced state from church and also fostered very close cooperation between civil and religious authorities. Fourth, some ministers also

---

45. Ibid., 155.
46. Ibid., 134.
47. E.g. Joshua Moodey, *Souldiery spiritualized* (Cambridge, 1674).
48. Thomas Watson, *Heaven taken by storm, or, The holy violence a Christian* (London, 1670), front matter–9.
49. Jewel House, Tower of London [RCIN 31729–310]).

served in political and military roles. The mid-1640s and 1650s saw an increasing martialisation of the ministry – and not simply because chaplains were in the armies. Shortly after Drogheda, Cromwell's chaplain, Hugh Peters, was given 'a Commission for a foot Regiment'.[50] Especially in the New Model Army – which came to be seen by some as a congregation – lay preaching by soldiers was permitted and often celebrated.

These four *occasions* facilitated the martialisation of spiritual warfare, but the *content* of sermons and treatises was also important. Ministers were very creative with making connections between physical and spiritual warfare. For example, the use of Ephesians 6:12 often shifted in conflict: 'For wee wrestle not [A] against flesh and blood, but [B] against principalities, against powers, against the rulers of the darknes of this world, against spirituall wickednes in high places'. In war, 'Not A but B' easily becomes 'By A then B'. Because the real war was spiritual, the human enemy might be treated as inconsequential. By striking the enemy, one struck the devil himself. The militant 'church militant' pierced through the chest of the enemy and into the heart of Satan. The enemy, a human, became a conduit.

Purity vs Unity

The New Testament held out several ideals for the church: Two are that they be unified and that they be pure. The Puritans, obviously, cared about purity. As with the other reformers, they also cared deeply about unity. However, unity and purity seemed to work against each other. A unified society is seldom ideologically or behaviourally pure. A society striving for purity is seldom unified. One of the most important works in the history of toleration – Roger Williams' *The Bloudy Tenent, of Persecution, for Cause of Conscience* (1644) – was structured as a dialogue between *Peace* and *Truth*. *Peace* and *Truth* were, as Williams framed it, best of friends who were seldom allowed to be together. It is unclear if Williams knew godly forces marched into battle with *Peace* and *Truth* emblazoned on some of their battle flags.[51]

---

50. Robert Ibbitson (pub.), *Severall proceedings in Parliament* (16th–23rd October, 1649) Issue 3: 23.
51. See examples in A. R. Young, *Emblematic Flag Devices of the English Civil*

A third ideal – in addition to a pure and unified church – was a church full of love. Love for brethren marked a disciple of Christ. However charity, historically speaking, was often a casualty in the pursuit of purity and truth. As illustrated in the discussion of the battle of Dunbar, the theology uttered against the Scots rivalled any other typological mixture produced on either side of the Atlantic. Presbyterians returned the ill will. Many on both sides fought for unity and purity. They reaped religious and political fragmentation. As communion gave way to conflict, brothers in Christ crossed the razor-thin line and became agents of Satan. As noted by Michael Winship, 'It was a frequent temptation... in puritan theological disputes to trace deviations from theological norms all the way to dire, deadly, and distant heresies'.[52] The godly adeptly remembered the blots on the family tree of opposing theological traditions, conveniently forgetting indecorous portions of their own.

The fiercest of fights were often between those with similar theology. This illustrates the latent potential for vehement quarrels with those who are *similar* to oneself. One can hate someone because they are an 'other' or despise them because they are a brother – and brothers know where all the fault lines are in the relationship. Sigmund Freud might consider Independent Puritan war with the Scots an example of the 'narcissism of small differences'. He noted the propensity of 'those communities that occupy contiguous territories and are otherwise related to each other' to 'indulge in feuding and mutual mockery'.[53] Theologians have made similar observations. In the words of Richard F. Lovelace, 'There seems to be a law of inverse cohesion among orthodox people, theologically analogous to the biological principle of territoriality: the closer two orthodox theologians get to one another's positions, the more reaction there is between them'.[54] Under some circumstances, it was far easier for the godly to tolerate unbelieving Native Americans living nearby than it was for them to tolerate someone with differing ecclesiology living in a neighbouring parish.

Wars 1642–1660 (Toronto: University of Toronto Press, 1995).

52. Winship, *Hot Protestants*, 106.

53. Sigmund Freud, *Civilization and Its Discontents* (Trans. David McLintock; London, 2002), 64.

54. Richard F. Lovelace, *Dynamics of Spiritual Life: An Evangelical Theology of Renewal* (Downers Grove: IVP Academic, 1979), 320, 322.

Many today feel indebted to Puritans for their theological insights. The temptation, then, is to refashion them in a modern image. It is important to recognise both continuity and discontinuity between historical persons and those who might have an affinity for them. Although many Protestants today might openly embrace the Puritans, it seems unlikely that this gesture would have been reciprocated. Most modern Protestants – even those steeped in Puritan theology – would have failed their test of purity and thus been excluded from unity.

'Othering' and 'Saming'

There are many ironies in the history of Christian political engagement. For example, this essay highlighted how attempts to uphold justice and treat life as sacred sometimes set in motion events that led to massacre. There are other ironies related to how the godly identified outsiders. As argued above, there was the danger of 'othering' an opponent who was very similar to oneself. On the flip side, there was also a danger in 'saming' the enemy. Violence can stem from viewing an 'other' as too *similar* to oneself; from assuming they share one's values and process for redressing grievances. The English were often unable or unwilling to view events from another's perspective.

Europeans held many beliefs about those they 'discovered' in the Americas. Like others, the godly sometimes spoke of enemies as devoid of morality (savage motif). At other points, they said that Algonquians were morally admirable though ignorant of Christianity (noble savage motif). Treating Native Americans as entirely different could create conflict. At other times, the godly treated them as very similar. This also fueled conflict, but for different reasons.

In *Virtuous Violence*, Alan Page Fiske and Tage Shakti Rai argue that in most cases of killing 'perpetrators are not morally disengaged; they are morally *engaged*. Victims are not dehumanized; they are *humanized*'.[55] For example, the godly seemed to view the Pequot both ways – as similar (when holding them common standards) and different (when prosecuting violations). The combination of these views proved fertile ground for confusion and conflict. The godly brought their conceptions

---

55. Fiske and Rai, *Virtuous Violence*, 159.

of morality into the combat zone. There they met enemies whom they thought were morally responsible for their injustice ('saming'). The injustice was defined from the perspective of the godly, and it was assumed that the enemy should naturally see their error ('saming'). Because they did not see their error, the unjust persons were now obstinate. They might actually lack characteristics common to civilised humans ('othering'). In the Pequot War, humanisation seems to have preceded dehumanisation.

5. Of Bombs and Balance

I have focused on one part of Puritan history, presenting an imbalanced portrait of them. I followed Puritans as they wielded weapons or justified the use of them – analysing some of their most controversial decisions, actions, and declarations. I described some of the darker moments of their history and explained how some of these controversial actions flowed from good intentions and admirable character traits. Much more of their story lies outside the frame provided here.

An imbalanced portrait can draw attention to what is often overlooked. As quoted earlier, Daniel Neal argued that later generations should remember 'the mistakes of our ancestors, when all the parties concerned are gone off the stage... [I]t may be of some use and benefit to mankind by enabling [us] to avoid those *rocks* on which [our] forefathers have split'. Many Christians have been slow to confess the role their traditions played in the development of racism, slow to critique the excessive violence that often accompanied missionary activity, slow to acknowledge the wrongs done in the name of God to Irish Catholics and Native Americans, and quick to idealize a golden age where politicians followed the Bible. This essay tries to problematise approaches to the past like this. John Owen, for example, was neither as pious as his most eloquent prose nor as hateful as his most vengeful sermon.[1] He was, more than anything, a complex individual who shaped his times and was shaped by them.[2]

The people discussed in this essay preferred to be called 'the godly'. The term 'Puritan' was purpose-built for ridicule.[3] The word stretched and morphed to cover a wide array of opinions and practices. The godly, however, were never woven of one fabric – except in the imaginations of some opponents. As the seventeenth century wore on, they came to resemble a coat of many colours or, at times, a patchwork of lumped

---

1. See quote above (Owen, *Advantage*, 16–17)
2. I refer the reader to two excellent biographies: Martyn C. Cowan, *John Owen and the Civil War Apocalypse: Preaching, Prophecy and Politics* (Abingdon: Routledge, 2018); Crawford Gribben, *John Owen and English Puritanism: Experiences of Defeat* (Oxford: Oxford University Press, 2016).
3. John Coffey and Paul C. H. Lim, 'Introduction', in John Coffey and Paul C. H. Lim (eds), *The Cambridge Companion to Puritanism* (Cambridge: Cambridge University Press, 2008), 1.

together temperaments and beliefs. Difficult to categorise, easy to caricature, the Puritan holds a privileged place in the cultural imagination. In fiction and film, Puritan virtues were commonly turned into vices even as their vices were accentuated and totalised. The term was famously defined by H. L. Mencken who said a Puritan was known by 'the haunting fear that someone, somewhere, may be happy'.[4]

The study of puritanism has come a long way since Mencken's biting remark. Many scholars challenge dour portraits of them. For example, in *Puritanism and the Pursuit of Happiness*, S. Bryn Roberts examined the ministry of Ralph Venning and demonstrated the centrality of happiness to his theology.[5] Puritan theology still has its defenders and detractors, with many Christians emphasising strands of this variegated tradition. The second half of the twentieth century witnessed a rising interest in Puritan theology that has continued into the present.[6]

It is not just conservative Christians who aim at revivification. In *Twenty-First Century Puritanism: Why We Need It and How It Can Help Us*, Stuart Sim mined Puritan history for beliefs, attitudes, and practices that could be secularised and repurposed. He had in mind 'Characteristics such as moral steadfastness, standing up for your beliefs, refusal to give in to political repression, respect for individual conscience and for learning, and dislike of hierarchy'. Secular puritanism provides a bulwark against 'anarchic libertarianism' and its 'depressingly cavalier attitude towards social responsibility and morality'.[7] Secular Puritans, Sim seems to suggest, would vote Democrat, Liberal Democrat or Labour.

Groups commonly leave a mixed legacy, and later generations might want to simplify their story so that their example can be adopted, adapted, or rejected. Historians highlight the complexities of the Puritan legacy. As John Coffey notes,

---

4. H. L. Mencken (ed.), *A Mencken Chrestomathy: His own Selection of His Choicest Writings* (New York: Vintage, 1982), 624.
5. S. Bryn Roberts, *Puritanism and the Pursuit of Happiness: The Ministry and Theology of Ralph Venning, c.1621–1674* (Woodbridge: Boydell, 2015), 5.
6. Leland Ryken, *J. I. Packer: An Evangelical Life* (Wheaton: Crossway, 2015), 268; cf. .263–79.
7. Stuart Sim, *Twenty-First Century Puritanism: Why We Need It and How It Can Help Us* (Champaign: Common Ground, 2018), 5–6.

'Puritanism has been credited (and blamed) for bequeathing a puzzling set of legacies, including the spirit of capitalism, scientific enterprise, Anglo-Saxon sexual repression, companionate marriage, liberal democracy, American exceptionalism and religious bigotry. Puritans have been hailed as midwives of modernity, and censured as reactionary foes of enlightened values'.[8]

Writing about political puritanism and warfare in the British Isles, he referred to 'the paradox of its bigotry and tolerance'.[9]

Scripture and theology played an important part in this variegated legacy. Christian beliefs had a multiplying effect on behaviours: The godly had greater reasons to forgive and also to demand justice; a stronger rationale for unity and more things to fight over; greater reasons to patiently submit to authority and more resources for rebellion; increased grounds for accepting responsibility and more arguments for shirking it; more reasons to fear shedding blood and more to justify it; more inspiration to conquer politics and more to withdraw from it. The godly, when pressured by politics, found verses and ideas in Scripture that pulled them towards opposite ways of living in the world. This is evidenced by the contradictory accusations levelled against Christianity, as noted by G. K. Chesterton: 'What could be the nature of the thing which one could abuse first because it would not fight, and second because it was always fighting?'[10]

How does this picture of political intoxication and righteous warriors fit with other portraits of sober divines and careful expositors of Scripture? Weighed in the balance, was political puritanism beneficial or detrimental to church or state? Timothy Samuel Shah provides a helpful way of remembering a complex past. In an introductory essay to the edited volumes *Christianity and Freedom*, Shah highlighted the ideas,

---

8. John Coffey, 'Puritan Legacies', in John Coffey and Paul C. H. Lim (eds), *The Cambridge Companion to Puritanism* (Cambridge: Cambridge University Press, 2008), 327.
9. Idem., *Persecution and Toleration in Protestant England, 1558–1689* (London: Pearson, 2000), 135.
10. G.K. Chesterton, *Orthodoxy*, in David Dooley (ed.), *The Collected Works of G. K. Chesterton* (San Francisco: Ignatius, 1986) I:291.

practices, and institutions that Christians bequeathed to the world. Our modern world, with its rights, representative governments, and rule of law, would be unthinkable without deep Christian reflection and involvement in politics.

Shah, however, was keenly aware of the darker side of the story. In emphasising the beneficial aspects, there was 'no revisionist intent to diminish the historical guilt of Christianity'. He also did not want to 'exaggerate Christianity's contributions to freedom and liberalism'. In these volumes, the contributors presented 'another story that needs to be told'. Shah's positive

> 'story in no way cancels out or even qualifies the record of Christian cruelties. It does not exculpate, exonerate, or even explain Christianity's sins, whether of omission or commission. It does not seek to "balance" the moral ledger, if that were even possible, for it has been well said that "the blood of one man shed by the hand of his brother, is too much for all ages, and for the whole earth". This other story is one that simply deserves to be set alongside the now more familiar story of Christian-inspired religious persecution and intolerance'.[11]

The picture I have presented here, this story of political intoxication 'in no way cancels out' other facets of Puritan history. However, this critique 'deserves to be set alongside' more positive narratives. The pursuit of power changed Puritan theology, often in ways that went unnoticed. This should encourage sobriety among those thirsting for power.

---

11. Timothy Samuel Shah, 'The Roots of Religious Freedom in Early Christian Thought', in Timothy Samuel Shah and Allen D. Hertzke (eds), *Christianity and Freedom* (Cambridge: Cambridge University Press, 2016) I:35.

If you have enjoyed this book, you might like to consider:

- supporting the work of the Latimer Trust
- reading more of our publications
- recommending them to others

See www.latimertrust.org for more information.

Ours is a True Church of God by *Donald John MacLean*

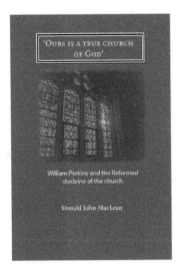

How do we discern a "true" church? Given the current ecclesiastical climate this is an increasingly pressing question. This study looks at how William Perkins, a great seventeenth century Church of England theologian, responded to this issue. Particular focus is given to his understanding of the distinctions between the visible and invisible church, and the marks of a "true" church, namely, word, sacraments and discipline. Judged against these marks, Perkins argued passionately that the Church of England was "a true church of God".

He also, in line with traditional Reformed ecclesiology, allowed significant doctrinal and practical decline before a church ceased to be a "true" church. The criteria he outlined for leaving a church amounted to nothing less than the obstinate and persistent overthrow of cardinal Christian doctrine and worship.

Perkins' careful teaching calls us to consider our response to declension in the church today. Ultimately his ecclesiology calls us to have a high view of the unity of the visible church, and in many causes to labour for recovery rather than to leave.

And the Light Shineth in Darkness by Kirsten Birkett

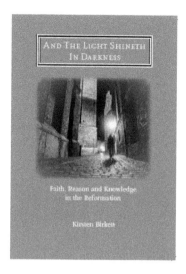

The Bible describes a fallen world and fallen humanity, in which minds are darkened. We reject God, and suppress the truth about him. How, then, can we know him at all? In other words, what are the noetic effects of sin? During the Reformation, doctrines of total depravity and the effects of the fall on the whole person re-emerged, with consequent implications for epistemology. If minds are fallen, how can we expect to know anything accurately? The purpose of this study is to start to answer that question by looking at some of the epistemology we find emerging from the writings of John Calvin and Martin Luther.

Portrait of a Prophet by *Martyn Cowan*

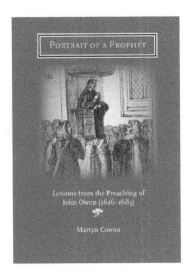

This study offers a sketch of John Owen's prophetic preaching in which his dogmatic providentialism and the fiery apocalypticism almost threaten to destroy his image as a Reformed Orthodox theologian and man of the Renaissance. With an initial glance, one might think that there is little practical to be learned from such a vignette. However, upon closer inspection three striking applications, or, in the language of early-modern homiletics, 'uses', emerge that are directly relevant for much contemporary preaching.